AF228218

MOTOCROSS

Written by Paul Stevenson

CONTENTS

This is Motocross!   4

Motocross History   6

Mighty Machines   8

The Bike   10

It's Tough   12

Safety Gear   14

The Race   16

Speed and Skill   18

The Finish   20

Supercross   22

Jumps   24

Freestyle   26

Tricks   28

Be a Racer   30

Glossary   31

Index   32

First published in 2024 by
Hungry Tomato Ltd
F15, Old Bakery Studios,
Blewetts Wharf, Malpas Road,
Truro, Cornwall,
TR1 1QH, UK.

Copyright © 2024 Hungry Tomato Ltd

A CIP catalog record for this book is available from
the British Library.

ISBN 9781915461902
Manufactured in the USA

Discover more at
www.hungrytomato.com

DISCLAIMER:

The moves and stunts
featured in this book
have been performed by
experienced, highly-trained
motocross riders. Do not,
under any circumstances,
try them yourself.

All words in **BOLD** can be found in the glossary.

This is... MOTOCROSS!

Motocross is one of the most exciting sports in the world.

Around 30 riders, on special motorcycles, race against each other.

Riders race on dirt tracks in open country. A motocross track is usually between 1 and 3 miles long.

The track includes huge hills and **drops**. There are fast, bumpy **straights** and tight corners.

There are also BIG JUMPS!

MOTOCROSS HISTORY

The first motocross races took place in the 1940s.

Special bikes were built for motocross from old road motorcycles.

The first motocross tracks didn't have many jumps because the bikes were heavy and not very strong. Also, the bikes had very poor **acceleration**, but on a straight, the bikes could go at 81 miles per hour.

Tracks were built to be as fast as possible.

THEY HAD LOTS OF STRAIGHTS AND FAST CORNERS!

The first motocross bikes were made entirely of metal
Early bikes were very heavy – some were double the weight of modern-day bikes!

MIGHTY MACHINES

Over the years, motocross bikes have developed more powerful engines.

They have tougher **suspension** and are much lighter. Modern bikes are made from lightweight aluminum and tough plastic.

This means the tracks can be rougher! They have more jumps and bigger jumps.

Modern tracks test the rider to the limit!

A huge selection of tracks in the sunshine state of California (USA) makes it the number one place where motocross riders from all over the world want to be racing.

THE BIKE

Motocross bikes are very different from normal motorcycles. The engines are built for power and speed.

The KTM 450 SX-F is one of the most powerful motocross bikes. It has a top speed of 123 mph.

It has four **gears**.

There is suspension at the front and back on most motocross bikes. This soaks up the impact of the big jumps and rough bumps on the track.

Tires with a chunky **tread** help the bike to grip the loose dirt.

Slim bodywork
Tough suspension
YAMAHA

IT'S TOUGH!

Motocross is one of the toughest sports in the world. Riders must train hard.

RIDERS MUST BE FIT AND STRONG TO COMPETE!

Spectacular crashes happen often

Pfei
Kawas
49
Cédric M
20

SAFETY GEAR

Riders wear lots of special gear and clothing when they race to keep them safe.

A helmet protects the head in a crash, and stops dirt and rocks from hitting the face. Large goggles protect the eyes.

Riders must wear motocross gear specifically designed for the sport; pants, jersey, gloves, a chest and back protector/body armor and a neck brace.

Motocross gear is made of materials that are tough but light. The rider can still move easily but is protected from flying dirt and crashes.

Knee and elbow pads protect riders in a fall.

Riders wear leather boots with hard plastic protectors.

THE RACE

Racers live for the time they line up for the start of a race.

RIDERS ARE HELD AT THE START GATES AND ARE SHOWN A "15 SECONDS LEFT TO GO" BOARD!

WHEN THE "5 SECONDS" STARTER BOARD IS SHOWN, THEIR BIKES ARE IN GEAR READY FOR THE GATES TO DROP!

SCRAMBLE FOR THE LEAD!

The bikes must pull through the deep dirt.
This is the most exciting and dangerous part of the race.

The racers charge into the first turn together

SPEED AND SKILL

The early stages of a race are frantic. Riders fight over top positions.

Only the best riders are able to attack the track and different jumps at full speed.

Riders out in front can control a race.

THE FINISH

Races, usually two laps, last about 30 minutes. The track gets pretty churned up.

Riders will be both physically and mentally tired.

This is where fitness counts; it's what riders train so hard for.

For some riders, tiredness means they come off their bikes and crash out of the race!

WHAT DOES IT TAKE TO WIN?

- Focus
- Energy
- Strength
- Talent
- Skill
- Bravery

GOOD LUCK!

SUPERCROSS

Supercross is a more spectacular form of motocross racing.

It takes place on specially built tracks, inside big stadiums.

Supercross is all about huge jumps and tight turns. These make the races intense and exciting for the huge crowds.

The races are short and action-packed. Racers have to ride very hard to overtake and get a good finish. Supercross can be very dangerous!

JUMPS

Supercross jumps need perfect timing.

The jumps give riders lots of chances to overtake and move into a better leaderboard position. As they fly over the jumps, riders try to take a better route than their rivals and get ahead of them.

Long sections of jumps are called "**rhythm sections**". The closely spaced bumps are known as "**whoops**".

This is a big triple jump.
Triple jumps throw riders high
into the air side by side.

FREESTYLE

Freestyle is the most extreme type of motocross. It's also the most dangerous.

Riders do not race in freestyle. Instead, they perform giant leaps and amazing tricks on their bikes.

Freestyle is thrilling and attracts big crowds

They do these giant leaps on specially built ramps, or off huge natural jumps and hills.

TRICKS

Good freestyle riders often do more than one trick as they fly through the air.

Here, a freestyle rider performs two tricks at once. This move is called a Seat Grab Hart Attack.

SEAT GRAB

A Seat Grab is when a rider grabs hold of the bike's saddle.

HART ATTACK

A Hart Attack is when a rider throws their legs into the air above their head. This trick was invented by rider Carey Hart.

A rider flips upside down as he performs the **backflip**.
This is one of the hardest and most dangerous freestyle tricks of all.
Only the best riders can tackle this move.

FREESTYLE REALLY IS INCREDIBLE!

BE A RACER

Getting started in motocross is easier than you think.

Each week, boys and girls line up together all over the world to ride and compete in races. Kids can start to learn from as young as 3 years old!

GLOSSARY

acceleration - the rate at which a vehicle increases its speed.

backflip - a backward somersault done in the air.

drop - a steep slope from the top of a hill. Drops make the track more challenging.

gears - the mechanical parts of a bike. They help it to accelerate. They also produce more power when powering up for jumps.

rhythm sections - long sections of jumps with different sized spaces in between.

straight - the fastest section of a motocross track. Straights are not long, but they are difficult to ride. This is because the ground is so rough that the riders must hang on tight.

suspension - the suspension is one of the most important parts of a motocross bike. It acts like a cushion so the riders don't feel all the bumps of the track. It also helps the tires grip the track.

tread - the surface of a tire. The tread on motocross tires has thick rubber blocks. They dig into the dirt to push the bike forward and stop the wheels slipping.

triple jump - when riders jump a huge distance in the air over a jump that features three dirt ramps in a row. The best riders jump all three ramps in one go.

whoops - a section of track that features a long series of big man-made bumps. The riders attack them at speed so they can skim across the top of the bumps.

INDEX

A
acceleration 6, 31
armor 15

B
backflip 29, 31
bikes 4, 6-7, 8-9, 10-11
bodywork 11
boots 15

C
corners 5, 6
crashes 12, 14-15, 21

D
drops 5, 31

E
engines 8, 10

F
freestyle 26-27, 28-29

G
gears (bike) 10, 31
goggles 14

H
Hart Attack 28
Hart, Carey 28
helmet 14
hills 5, 27
history 6-7, 9

J
jumps 5, 6, 9, 10, 19, 23, 24-25, 27
jerseys 15

K
knee pads 15
KTM 450 SX-F 10-11

O
overtaking 23, 24

R
races 6, 9, 20, 22-23, 30
ramps 27
rhythm sections 24, 31

S
saddle 28
safety gear 14-15
Seat Grab 28
Seat Grab Hart Attack 28
stadiums 22-23
straights 5, 6, 31
supercross 22-23, 24
suspension 9, 10-11, 31

T
tracks 5, 6, 9, 19, 20, 22-23
tread 10, 31
tricks 26, 28-29
triple jumps 25, 31
turns 23
tires 10

W
whoops 24, 31

Picture credits:

(t=top; b=bottom; c=center; l=left; r=right):
Shutterstock: 1, 8, 14, 15, 17, 18, 19, 20, 21t, 31t, 31b; Edu_2ev 30tl; Jan.Melichar 28c; Master1305 30b; Sippakorn 16c; Sonrak 9c. 2DPPI/ Actionplus: 29. Aris Messinis/ AFP/ Getty Images: 25. Ben Johnson: 10-11. Imagebroker/ Alamy: 24b. Martin Meissner/ AP/ PA Photos: 12-13. Phil Rees/ Rex Features: 22-23. Shelly Castellano/ Icon SMI/ Corbis: 26-27. Sherman/ Getty Images: 6-7. Steve Bardens/ actionplus: 4-5, 21bl.

Every effort has been made to trace the copyright holders, and we apologize in advance for any unintentional omissions. We would be pleased to insert the appropriate acknowledgments in any subsequent edition of this publication.